BOOKSMITH JOURNAL BOOKSMITH PRESS

BOOKSMITH PUBLISHING

seattle, washington

Booksmith Press

Inspiring creative minds, one book at a time.

Explore more illustrated journals, books, and other aesthetic gifts:

WWW.BOOKSMITH.IO

BPNB 1 | ISBN 978-1-73597-254-1

Cover image inspired by Paweł Czerwiński

Booksmith Publishing | Seattle, Washington

www.ingramcontent.com/pod-product-compliance
Ingram Content Group UK Ltd.
Pitfield, Milton Keynes, MK11 3LW, UK
UKHW060118010826
14089UKWH00004B/48

9 781735 972541